°F (Fahrenhei...	
32 (water freezes)	0
200	95
212 (water boils)	100
250	120
300	150
350 (moderate oven)	175
400 (hot oven)	205
450 (very hot oven)	230
500 (extremely hot oven)	260

L E N G T H S

U.S. Measurements	Metric Equivalents
1/4 inch	6 mm
1/2 inch	1.2 cm
3/4 inch	2 cm
1 inch	2.5 cm
2 inches	5 cm
5 inches	12.5 cm

SALSAS

**Andrews McMeel
Publishing**

Kansas City

www.andrewsmcmeel.com

ISBN: 0-8362-5230-6

Library of Congress Catalog Card Number: 97-74527

First U.S. Edition

1 2 3 4 5 6 7 8 9 10

Editor: Deborah Mintcheff
Designer: Yolanda Monteza
Photographer: Steven Mark Needham
Illustrator: Ed Lam

Produced by Smallwood & Stewart, Inc., New York City

TABLE OF CONTENTS

S A L S

It is not surprising that salsas have over-taken ketchup as America's number-one condiment. Salsas are easy to prepare, low in calories and fat, and fun to dip into. Best of all, they can be served with almost any meat, fish, poultry, or vegetable and brighten up even the simplest food. Salsa and a basket of freshly made tortilla chips is the perfect accompaniment for ice-cold beer or frosty margaritas.

Salsas, along with grilled food and

homemade tortillas, are one of the fundamental elements of Mexican cooking. In that country, the fruits, vegetables, chiles, herbs, and spices of each region are reflected in its salsas. These fresh, colorful dishes are ideal for the warm weather.

In its simplest form, a salsa consists of a base ingredient such as fresh or roasted tomatoes, avocados, tomatillos, or a fruit such as pineapple or melon. Fresh or roasted chiles, onions or scallions, and some fresh or dried herbs contribute complexity. It's that simple.

If, until now, supermarket salsas have been the limit of your salsa-eating experience, you are in for a real treat. Included in this compact but comprehensive guide is a detailed description of the twelve most common salsa ingredients. For easy reference, the recipe section is divided into three chapters: tomato salsas, vegetable salsas, and fruit salsas.

Ultimately, what a salsa is composed of is meant to be flexible. If you desire more herbs, spices, or heat, add whatever is your preference. Salsas are easygoing. The basic idea remains the same—salsas have deliciously intense flavors that will have you coming back for more. There is no doubt that once you start making your own salsas rather than purchasing them, you'll be hooked.

SALSA INGREDIENTS

CHIPOTLE: The chipotle chile is a dried and smoked red jalapeño chile. Its name is derived from the Indian words *chil* (chile) and *poctli* (smoke). Chipotle chiles are coffee colored, wrinkled, and two to four inches long. Their complex smoky flavor marries well with most foods. On the heat scale, chipotles are considered hot. They are also available canned in adobo sauce—a heady blend of tomato, vinegar, onion, and spices.

CILANTRO: Cilantro, also known as fresh coriander, is an aromatic annual herb native to the Mediterranean. Its leaves, roots, and stems have been prized for over three thousand years. Cilantro leaves are an integral part of Chinese, Indian, and Thai cooking. If you haven't used cilantro before, try it in small amounts. Cilantro combines especially well with fresh parsley and mint and adds a refreshing note to both sweet and savory salsas.

CITRUS: Lime and lemon juice lend a tangy note to salsas. Their sweet-tart flavor can lift and brighten both vegetable and fruit salsas. When choosing lemons and limes, pick fruit that is firm and heavy for its size, with close-grained, glossy skin. Fruit with smooth, thin skin has more juice than those with thick skin. To get the most juice out of lemons or limes, first roll them under your palms using a little pressure, then halve and juice.

GARLIC: Garlic has been cultivated for over five thousand years, making it one of the oldest farmed plants. Garlic is made up of a "head," sometimes called a bulb, which consists of individual cloves covered with a thin papery skin. There are over thirty varieties of garlic—the most readily available are the white, pink, and purple varieties. When choosing garlic, look for very firm, plump heads with large cloves.

GINGER: Ginger is the underground rhizome of a tropical plant. Contrary to some opinion, it is not a root and is called gingerroot incorrectly. When buying ginger, select pieces that are firm, plump, and wrinkle-free. To store ginger, peel and thinly slice it. Place the slices in a jar and cover with Chinese rice wine or dry sherry. Seal the jar and refrigerate for up to several months.

JALAPEÑO: The jalapeño is the best-known and most widely used fresh chile. It is named after the town of Jalapa in the Mexican state of Veracruz. On the heat scale, jalapeños register medium-hot. Unripe, they are dark green, but when allowed to ripen, they turn bright red. Red jalapeños are slightly sweeter than the green—when they are dried and smoked, they are called chipotle chiles.

ONION: Onions have been prized for over five thousand years. The variety we use most often in cooking is the yellow globe onion—it has a strong flavor which makes it ideal for robust dishes. Spanish onions are very large and known for their mild, sweet flavor. Red onions have a slightly sweet flavor and a crisp texture. Their color makes them a good addition to salsas.

PARSLEY: Parsley is an aromatic biennial herb that is either flat-leaf or curly. The flat-leafed variety is the more flavorful and is used more often in cooking. Parsley's cool and refreshing flavor is a welcome addition to salsas. It can be sprinkled on as a garnish or added in generous quantities to contribute both flavor and color.

SCALLION: First grown in south-western Siberia, scallions have been cultivated for two thousand years. Both the white and green parts are edible, although a recipe will sometimes utilize only one part. Scallions have long hollow green "leaves," and can grow up to two feet in length. The white stems are sometimes partially covered with soil to encourage growth. Buy scallions that are plump with firm green tops.

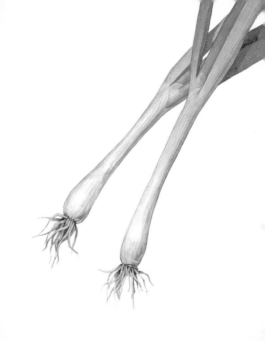

SERRANOS: Serranos are short, slender fresh chiles that rate very hot on the heat scale. Serranos are sold both green and red—the red is riper and therefore sweeter than the green. Perhaps the most common use of serranos is in fresh salsas, but it is also the chile that is most often pickled (*en escabeche*) and enjoyed as a snack or hors d'oeuvre in Mexico.

TOMATILLOS: Tomatillos are members of the nightshade family along with eggplants, tomatoes, potatoes, and peppers. They resemble small, hard green tomatoes covered with a thin papery husk. Tomatillos can be eaten either raw or cooked. Choose those that are very firm and without any yellowing. Remove the husks and thoroughly wash them under cold water to remove the sticky coating on the skin.

TOMATOES: There are more than a thousand varieties of tomatoes—the most common are the red, plum (also known as Roma), cherry, pear, yellow, green, and currant tomatoes. Their flavor depends on the degree of acidity, sugar content, water content, and at what point they are harvested during the growing season. Almost any tomato can be used in a salsa, and the different kinds can be combined for visual and flavor interest.

R E C I

P E S

Salsa Cruda

The success of this simple salsa depends on using fruity extra-virgin olive oil and the ripest tomatoes you can find. You can offer it as a dip, perhaps with the addition of a bit of diced avocado. Served with warmed flour tortillas and hot-off-the-grill shrimp, this is a real summertime treat.

3 long green chiles, such as New Mexico, or 1 (4-ounce) can whole green chiles, drained

3 large tomatoes (about 1$^{1}/_{2}$ pounds), chopped

16 large fresh basil leaves, shredded

2 garlic cloves, minced

2 tablespoons extra-virgin olive oil

Salt and freshly ground pepper

Over a gas flame or under a broiler, roast the fresh chiles, turning them often, for 3 to 4 minutes, until the skin is blistered and brown. Put the chiles into a plastic bag, seal tightly, and steam for 10 minutes.

When the chiles are cool enough to handle, peel, core, and seed. Chop the chiles and transfer them to a medium bowl.

Stir in the tomatoes, basil, garlic, and oil, and season with salt and pepper. Stir until well mixed. Cover the salsa and set aside for 30 minutes to allow the flavors to blend. *Makes about 4 cups*

Tomato-Chile Salsa

The ingredients for this cooked tomato salsa are gently simmered, which blends and softens the flavors. The cumin seeds are toasted before being ground to intensify their delicious, exotic flavor.

2 (28-ounce) cans whole tomatoes

1½ teaspoons cumin seeds

⅓ cup vegetable or olive oil

1¾ cups chopped onions

2 large garlic cloves, minced

2 or 3 chiles de árbol, crushed,
    or 1 to 2 teaspoons
    crushed red pepper flakes

1 teaspoon dried oregano

2 bay leaves

Salt

In a food processor, coarsely puree the tomatoes, in batches, with their juice. Transfer the puree to a large bowl and set aside.

In a small skillet, toast the cumin seeds over medium-low heat, stirring often, for 2 to 3 minutes, until fragrant. With a mortar and pestle or in a spice grinder, pound or grind the seeds to form a powder. Transfer to a small dish; set aside.

In a large nonreactive saucepan, heat the oil over medium-high heat. Cook the onions and garlic, stirring often, for about 5 minutes, or until the onions are softened. Add the tomatoes, chiles, oregano, cumin, and bay leaves, stirring until combined. Reduce the heat to low and simmer, stirring frequently, for 35 to 45 minutes, until the salsa is rich-tasting and thickened to the consistency of tomato sauce. Season with salt.

Remove the salsa from the heat and discard the bay leaves. Cool to room temperature before serving. The salsa can be stored in the refrigerator in a covered container up to 1 week.

Makes about 6 cups

Blackened Tomato and Olive Salsa

If you are already firing up your grill, it's worth it to grill the tomatoes for this savory salsa—their flavor will become rich and concentrated. For a quick supper, serve the salsa spooned over grilled chicken breasts or pasta.

6 plum tomatoes

$1/3$ cup coarsely chopped brine-cured
   black olives

6 roasted large garlic cloves, peeled*

2 tablespoons toasted pine nuts
   (see Note p. 54)

1 tablespoon chopped fresh basil

1 tablespoon chopped fresh cilantro

1 tablespoon olive oil

1 tablespoon fresh lemon juice

1 tablespoon red wine vinegar

1 teaspoon crushed red pepper flakes

$1/4$ teaspoon salt

$1/8$ teaspoon freshly ground pepper

*To roast garlic, wrap the cloves in foil and roast
in a 375°F oven for about 25 minutes, or until
softened.

Preheat a gas grill to medium-high, a charcoal grill to medium-hot, or preheat the broiler.

Grill or broil the tomatoes, turning them several times, for about 10 minutes, or until the skins are blackened on all sides. Transfer to a plate and when cool enough to handle, peel and cut the tomatoes into $1/2$-inch chunks.

Put the tomatoes into a medium bowl. Add the remaining ingredients, stirring until well mixed. Cover the salsa and refrigerate for at least 30 minutes or up to several hours before serving. *Makes about $2^{1}/2$ cups* 🔴

Avocado and Basil Salsa

This unusual salsa combines the buttery taste of avocado with flavorful sun-dried tomatoes and fragrant basil. Add this salsa to bean burritos, or spoon it onto thinly sliced, toasted French bread and serve as an hors d'oeuvre accompanied by white wine.

¹/₄ cup oil-packed sun-dried tomatoes,
    drained and chopped

1 plum tomato, cut into ¹/₄-inch dice

2 tablespoons chopped fresh basil

1 jalapeño chile, seeded and minced

1 large garlic clove, minced

2 tablespoons fresh lemon juice

¹/₄ teaspoon salt

1 large ripe Hass avocado, halved,
    pitted, peeled, and cut into
    ¹/₄-inch dice

In a medium bowl, put the sun-dried tomatoes, plum tomato, basil, jalapeño, garlic, lemon juice, and salt, and stir until combined. Add the avocado, gently stirring until mixed.

Cover the salsa and refrigerate for at least 30 minutes or up to 4 hours. For the best flavor, let the salsa come to room temperature before serving. *Makes 1¹/₂ cups*

Guacamole

In a medium bowl, put 1 ripe Hass avocado, halved, pitted, peeled, and cut into $1/2$-inch chunks. Using a fork, roughly mash the avocado, leaving lots of chunks. Add 1 medium tomato, chopped; 1 small onion, finely chopped; 1 small jalapeño chile, seeded and finely chopped; 1 to 2 tablespoons fresh lime juice; and salt and pepper to taste, stirring until mixed. Stir in about $1/3$ cup chopped fresh cilantro if desired. Serve immediately, or cover and refrigerate for up to several hours. *Makes about 2 cups*

Lemon-Herb Salsa

Seeds, nuts, and herbs have been added to condiments for centuries. Here, pumpkin seeds are combined with fresh herbs, lemon zest, and ripe yellow tomatoes. The result is a pungent, zesty salsa that is an ideal accompaniment for seafood, pork, chicken, pasta, or vegetables.

$^1/_4$ cup pumpkin seeds, toasted
    (see Note)
2 garlic cloves, halved
$^1/_4$ cup coarsely chopped fresh
    flat-leaf parsley
2 tablespoons chopped fresh basil
2 tablespoons chopped fresh rosemary
$^1/_4$ cup extra-virgin olive oil
2 tablespoons grated lemon zest
2 tablespoons fresh lemon juice
1 large yellow tomato, chopped
$^1/_2$ teaspoon salt
Freshly ground pepper

Note: To toast, put them into a small skillet
and toast over medium-high heat, stirring, for
3 minutes, or until golden.

In a food processor, process the pumpkin seeds until a chunky paste forms. Add the garlic and process until almost smooth. Add the parsley, basil, and rosemary, processing until smooth.

Transfer the mixture to a medium bowl and whisk in the olive oil, lemon zest, and lemon juice until incorporated. Gently stir in the tomato and season with the salt and pepper to taste. Cover the salsa and refrigerate for at least 1 hour or up to 1 day before serving. For the best flavor, bring to room temperature before serving. *Makes about 2 cups*

Red Pepper and Ginger Salsa

Hot chili oil is made from toasted sesame oil that is infused with dried red chiles, which turn the oil a brilliant orange. It is available in Asian markets and many supermarkets.

3 large red bell peppers, roasted, peeled,
      cored, seeded, and cut into
      thin strips (see Note p. 58)
1 scallion (green part only), thinly sliced
2 tablespoons chopped peeled
      fresh ginger
2 garlic cloves, minced
2 tablespoons Asian hot chili oil
2 tablespoons rice wine vinegar
$1/2$ teaspoon sugar
$1/2$ teaspoon salt
1 tablespoon sesame seeds
1 tablespoon coarsely chopped fresh
      cilantro, for garnish

In a medium bowl, combine the bell peppers, scallion, ginger, garlic, oil, vinegar, sugar, and salt, tossing until well mixed. Cover and refrigerate up to two days.

To serve, bring the salsa to room temperature, stir in the sesame seeds, and sprinkle with the cilantro. *Makes 2¹/₂ cups*

Note: To roast bell peppers, put them under the broiler or over a gas or charcoal flame for 15 minutes, or until blackened on all sides. Put the peppers into a plastic bag, seal tightly, and steam for 10 minutes.

Pan-Roasted Corn and Chipotle Salsa

Pan-roasting fresh corn gives it a nutty flavor that goes well with the smoky-hot flavor of chipotle chiles. Chipotle chiles in adobo sauce are available in specialty food stores.

2 ears fresh corn, silk and husks
   removed and kernels cut off

3 plum tomatoes, chopped

4 chipotle chiles in adobo sauce, coarsely
   chopped, plus 2 tablespoons
   adobo sauce

3 tablespoons chopped fresh cilantro

2 tablespoons finely chopped red onion

4 garlic cloves, minced

1 tablespoon chopped fresh
   flat-leaf parsley

$1/4$ teaspoon salt

$1/4$ cup sherry vinegar

$1/4$ cup cold water

Heat a large heavy skillet over high heat until hot. Add the corn, spreading it in an even layer, and cook, stirring often, for 4 to 5 minutes, until the corn is tender and some of the kernels are nicely browned.

Transfer the corn to a medium bowl and add the tomatoes, chipotles and adobo sauce, the cilantro, onion, garlic, parsley, salt, vinegar, and water, stirring until well mixed.

Cover the salsa and refrigerate until ready to serve. This salsa will keep up to 3 days.

Makes 3 cups

Salsa Verde

When buying tomatillos, choose bright green, firm ones without yellowing or soft spots. As delicious as this salsa is with crisp tortilla chips, it's equally luscious served alongside grilled chicken or fish.

1^1/$_2$ pounds tomatillos, husked and
    well washed

1^1/$_4$ cups chopped onions

4 large garlic cloves, minced

3 or 4 jalapeño chiles, halved
    and seeded

3 tablespoons olive oil

1 teaspoon salt, or more to taste

^{1}/$_2$ teaspoon freshly ground pepper,
    or more to taste

^{1}/$_2$ cup coarsely chopped fresh cilantro

Preheat the oven to 450°F. In a shallow baking dish, combine the tomatillos, onions, garlic, chiles, oil, salt, and pepper. Roast, stirring occasionally, for 30 minutes, or until the onions are golden. Remove from the oven and set aside until room temperature.

Transfer the tomatillo mixture to a food processor; process until coarsely chopped. Add the cilantro and process, pulsing, until mixed. Season to taste with salt and pepper if necessary. Transfer to a container and refrigerate up to three days. *Makes 3¹/₂ cups*

Roasted Eggplant and Red Pepper Salsa

The Chinese make vinegars from rice, wheat, peaches, and grapes. Black vinegar is made from fermented rice. It has a distinctive dark color and an intense flavor. It is available in Asian markets and many supermarkets.

2 medium Japanese eggplants
  (about 1 pound)
2 large red bell peppers
1 cup chopped fresh cilantro
2 garlic cloves, minced
1 tablespoon finely chopped peeled
  fresh ginger
1/4 cup Chinese black vinegar or
  balsamic vinegar
2 tablespoons Asian sesame oil
1 tablespoon Asian hot chili oil
2 teaspoons sugar
2/3 cup chopped scallions
1 teaspoon salt

Preheat the oven to 400°F.

Prick the eggplants with a fork and put onto a baking sheet with the bell peppers.

Bake for 20 minutes, or until the vegetables are very soft. Put the peppers into a plastic bag, seal tightly, and steam for 10 minutes. Set the eggplants aside until cool enough to handle.

Peel, core, seed, and chop the peppers. Put them into a large bowl. Peel and chop the eggplants and add to the bowl along with the remaining ingredients, mixing well. Let the salsa sit at room temperature for about 1 hour to allow the flavors to blend. The salsa can be refrigerated up to three days. *Makes 3 cups*

Grilled Pineapple and Jícama Salsa

Jícama quickly loses its crisp texture when combined with ripe pineapple, so plan to serve this delectable salsa freshly made. It pairs equally well with chicken, pork, and seafood.

$^1/_2$ pineapple, peeled, cored, and cut
    into $^1/_2$-inch-thick slices

1$^1/_2$ cups coarsely grated peeled jícama

1 teaspoon rice wine vinegar

$^1/_2$ teaspoon honey

$^1/_4$ teaspoon cumin seeds, toasted
    (see Note p. 54)

Pinch of salt

$^1/_4$ teaspoon coarsely ground pepper

Fresh cilantro leaves, for garnish
    (optional)

Preheat a grill to medium-high.

Grill the pineapple for 1 to 2 minutes per side, until nicely marked and slightly softened. Remove from the grill and when cool enough to handle, cut the pineapple into ½-inch cubes and put into a large bowl.

Add the jícama, rice vinegar, honey, cumin seeds, salt, and pepper, stirring until well mixed. Spoon into a dish, sprinkle with cilantro leaves if using, and serve. *Makes 3 cups*

Red Grapefruit
and Mint Salsa

Fresh Thai chiles, also called bird chiles, are among the hottest. You may find serrano chiles easier to locate and they make a fine substitute. Despite its intense heat, this salsa is refreshing. Serve alongside chicken.

1 large red grapefruit

2 red Thai or serrano chiles, minced

2 tablespoons minced shallots

2 tablespoons lightly packed fresh cilantro leaves

1 teaspoon chopped fresh mint

3 tablespoons fresh lime juice

With a serrated knife, cut a slice from the top and bottom of the grapefruit, cutting through to the flesh. Cutting from top to bottom, slice away the peel and pith from the grapefruit, following the natural curve of the fruit. To remove the grapefruit in sections, slide the knife down along one side of each segment, separating the flesh from the membrane. Cut down along the other side of the segment and remove it.

Put the grapefruit segments into a medium bowl along with the chiles, shallots, cilantro, mint, and lime juice, gently stirring until mixed. Serve immediately or refrigerate up to several hours. *Makes 1¹/2 cups*

Melon Salsa with Honey and Mint

This simple salsa is at its most tempting when freshly made. Prepare it at the height of the summer, and serve it with grilled or roasted pork or spooned over scoops of sorbet.

2 cups diced ($^1/_8$-inch) cantaloupe
    or other melon

1 teaspoon chopped fresh mint

1 tablespoon fresh lime juice

2 teaspoons honey

$^1/_4$ to $^1/_2$ teaspoon medium-hot pure
    chile powder (optional)

Pinch of salt

In a small bowl, combine the cantaloupe, mint, lime juice, honey, chile powder if using, and salt, gently stirring until well mixed. Cover and refrigerate for at least 1 or up to 6 hours.

Makes 2 cups

Cranberry-Lime Salsa

In a medium nonreactive saucepan, put a 12-ounce bag of fresh cranberries and cold water to cover. Bring to a boil over high heat. Cook for 2 minutes, or until the cranberries just begin to pop. Drain the cranberries.

In a large bowl, combine ½ cup sugar and ⅓ cup fresh lime juice, stirring until the sugar dissolves. Stir in the cranberries, ½ cup chopped fresh cilantro, 3 scallions, finely chopped, 1 jalapeño chile, seeded and minced, and 2 garlic cloves, minced. Season with salt. Let stand for 30 minutes before serving. *Makes 3 cups*

LIQUID MEASURES

Spoons and Cups	Metric Equivalents
½ tsp.	2.5 ml
1 tsp.	5 ml
1 Tbs. (3 tsp.)	15 ml
¼ cup	60 ml
⅓ cup	80 ml
½ cup	120 ml
1 cup (8 ounces)	240 ml
4 cups (1 quart)	950 ml
4 quarts (1 gallon)	3.8 liters

(tsp.: teaspoon/Tbs.: tablespoon)

WEIGHTS

Ounces and Pounds	Metric Equivalents
½ ounce	14 g
1 ounce	28 g
2 ounces	57 g
4 ounces (¼ pound)	113 g
8 ounces (½ pound)	225 g
16 ounces (1 pound)	454 g